TALHA SHARIF

CAREER TRIUMPH

AIM HIGH, LOCK & LOAD YOUR CAREER: SNIPER STRATEGIES FOR LANDING YOUR CAREER BULLSEYES

Chapter 1: Introduction to the Recruitment Process

Part 1: Demystifying the Recruitment Process

The process of finding and getting a job can often seem like a mysterious and complicated journey. However, it is necessary to first demystify the recruitment process. Understanding how recruiting works is the first step in finding your dream job.

Recruitment is the systematic process used by organizations to identify, attract, evaluate, and hire suitable candidates to fill job vacancies. It involves multiple stages and numerous stakeholders, including HR professionals, recruiting managers, and sometimes external recruiters. While each organization may have its own unique approach, the core principles of recruitment remain consistent.

The process typically begins with determining the need to fill a specific job position, whether due to growth or to replace a departing employee. Employers develop job descriptions and requirements that outline the skills and qualifications they seek in potential candidates. These job descriptions will form the basis of your job search. By understanding this early stage, you can tailor your application and strategy to meet the specific requirements of your target employer.

Part 2: The Recruiter's Role in the Job Search

Recruiters play a key role in your job search. They act as an intermediary between you, the job candidate, and the employer. Understanding their role can help you navigate the recruiting process more effectively.

Recruiters come in many forms. Internal recruiters work within the organizations they recruit from, while external or third-party recruiters are often employed by recruiting agencies to source talent for multiple clients. The primary responsibility of a recruiter is to identify, screen, and recommend the best candidates for the position.

They act as gatekeepers, screening resumes, conducting interviews and assessing candidates' qualifications. As a job seeker, you should view your recruiter as a valuable ally. They can provide insights into company culture, the interview process, and the specific skills or traits employers are looking for.

It can be advantageous to build relationships with recruiters in your field. They often have inside information about job openings, but this information may not be released publicly. By building a rapport with them, you'll increase your chances of being considered for a position that aligns with your career goals.

Part 3: Your Employment Journey

Your journey to employment is a unique and personal one. Start by setting clear career goals and understanding your motivations. Are you looking for a job that provides financial stability, career growth, or personal fulfillment? Your goals will guide your job search strategy.

This journey involves self-assessment, identifying your strengths, weaknesses, skills, and values. When crafting a compelling resume and cover letter, it's crucial to know yourself and what you bring to the table. It will also help you articulate your value during the interview.

The process is not always linear, and setbacks are a natural part of the journey. You may face rejection, and certain opportunities may not align with your goals. However, persistence, adaptability, and a positive mindset are your allies on this path. Remember, every step, including setbacks, helps you grow as a professional.

Your employment journey is also about a process of learning and continuous improvement. As you embark on this adventure, you'll gain valuable insights, gain new skills, and build a network. All of these experiences will contribute to your personal and professional development, ultimately bringing you closer to your dream job.

Chapter 2: Know Your Career Goals

Part 1: Self-assess and determine your goals

Understanding your career goals starts with a self-assessment. Take some time to reflect on your skills, interests, values, and desires. What is your favorite thing to do? What are you passionate about? What are your core values? What kind of work environment aligns with these values?

Self-assessment tools, personality tests, and career assessments may be helpful during this process. These resources provide a structured approach to discovering your strengths, weaknesses, and personality traits. They can also reveal potential career paths that would fit your profile. Tools like the Myers-Briggs Type Indicator (MBTI), StrengthsFinder, and Holland Code are popular choices.

Once you have a clearer understanding of yourself, you can begin to identify your career goals. What do you hope to achieve in your career in the short and long term? Your goals may include a specific job title, industry, income level, or personal development milestones. Be specific and realistic when setting goals. Your goals should serve as a roadmap for your career.

Part 2: Build your personal brand

Your personal brand is how you present yourself to the professional world. It is a combination of your skills, experience, values and unique qualities. Building a strong personal brand can help you stand out from other candidates and attract the right opportunities.

Start by crafting a clear elevator pitch. This is a brief summary of who you are and what you bring to the profession. It should communicate your unique value proposition to potential employers. Practice expressing it confidently as it will come in handy at networking events, interviews and even casual conversations.

Your personal brand also extends to your online presence. LinkedIn is a valuable platform for professionals to showcase their skills and network with industry peers. Make sure your LinkedIn profile is complete, including a professional photo, a compelling headline, a detailed summary, and recommendations from colleagues or supervisors.

Consider starting a personal website or blog to showcase your expertise and share your thoughts on industry trends. Not only does this demonstrate your knowledge, it also makes it easier for potential employers to discover you through online searches.

Part 3: Customize your career path

Once you've identified your goals and established a personal brand, you can customize your career path to fit your goals. This may involve identifying the skills and qualifications required for your desired role and looking for opportunities to gain these skills and qualifications.

Consider creating a career development plan that outlines the steps you need to take to achieve your goals. Break your goals down into smaller, manageable tasks and set deadlines to hold yourself accountable.

Networking is an important part of tailoring your career path. Building relationships with professionals in your industry can open doors to opportunities, mentorship, and valuable insights. Attend industry events, join relevant online forums, and connect with people who inspire you or work at your target companies.

Remember, your career path will evolve over time. It is critical to remain flexible and adapt to changing circumstances and new opportunities. By continually re-evaluating your goals and making adjustments as needed, you can ensure your career stays on the right track.

Chapter 3: Navigating the Job Market

Part 1: Explore job opportunities

Exploring job opportunities is a critical step in finding your dream job. The job market is a dynamic environment full of diverse opportunities, and it is important to search strategically.

Start by identifying your target company and industry. Research organizations that align with your career goals, values, and interests. Many employers provide information about their company culture, mission, and open positions on their websites. This knowledge can help you narrow your focus and find the best opportunities.

Job openings can be found in many places, including company websites, job boards, and professional associations. Attend job fairs, industry conferences, and local networking events to get first-hand knowledge of potential employers. Networking is often the key to uncovering hidden job opportunities, so don't underestimate the power of personal connections.

Part 2: Online Job Search and Networking

In today's digital age, online job search and networking play a key role in finding job opportunities. Job seekers have access to a wealth of online resources to assist in their search.

Start by creating a professional online presence. LinkedIn is a valuable platform to connect with professionals in your field. Make sure your LinkedIn profile is complete, including a professional photo, a compelling headline, a detailed summary, and recommendations from colleagues or supervisors.

Job search engines and aggregation sites such as Indeed, Glassdoor, and LinkedIn Jobs provide extensive listings of job opportunities. These platforms offer advanced search filters that allow you to narrow your choices based on factors such as location, industry, and job title. You can also set up job alerts to be notified when new jobs that match your criteria become available.

Consider exploring industry-specific job boards and forums. These professional resources target specific fields or careers, providing tailored job listings and opportunities to connect with like-minded professionals. Research industry publications, association websites, and forums to find the resources most relevant to your career.

Utilizing Linkedin

Using LinkedIn effectively for job searching, applying, and ultimately winning jobs is a strategic process. With over 700 million users, LinkedIn is a powerful platform for career advancement and job opportunities. Here's a comprehensive guide on how to make the most of LinkedIn in your job search:

Optimize Your LinkedIn Profile:

Complete Your Profile: Ensure your profile is 100% complete. This means adding a professional photo, a compelling headline, and a summary that highlights your skills, experience, and career goals.

Use Keywords: Incorporate relevant keywords related to your skills, industry, and job interests in your profile summary, job descriptions, and skills section. This will improve your visibility in search results.

Customize Your LinkedIn URL: Edit your public profile URL to include your name. This makes it easier to share your profile and enhances your personal brand.

Build a Professional Network: Connect with colleagues, classmates, mentors, and professionals in your field. The larger and more relevant your network, the more opportunities you'll discover.

Job Searching on LinkedIn:

Use the Jobs Tab: Utilize LinkedIn's "Jobs" tab to search for positions by job title, location, company, and other relevant filters. You can also set up job alerts to receive notifications about new job postings.

Follow Companies: Follow companies you're interested in to receive updates on their job openings and company news.

Leverage the "Easy Apply" Feature: Some job postings have an "Easy Apply" option, which simplifies the application process. Use this when applicable to increase your chances of being noticed.

Applying for Jobs:

Tailor Your Application: Customize your resume and cover letter for each job application. Highlight the skills and experiences that align with the specific job requirements.

Use the "Apply on Company Website" Option: When available, use this option as it often allows for more detailed application submissions. You can also express your interest directly through LinkedIn.

Networking and Engagement:

Engage with Content: Interact with posts, articles, and updates from your network and companies you're interested in. Commenting and sharing relevant content can help you stay visible and build relationships.

Message Recruiters: If you come across a job posting that aligns with your skills and interests, don't hesitate to reach out to the recruiter or hiring manager directly with a personalized message expressing your interest.

Join LinkedIn Groups: Participate in LinkedIn groups related to your industry or interests. Engaging in group discussions can help you connect with like-minded professionals and discover job opportunities.

Recommendations and Endorsements:

Seek Recommendations: Request recommendations from colleagues, supervisors, and mentors. These endorsements can provide credibility and showcase your skills.

Endorse Others: Endorsing the skills of your connections can encourage them to endorse your skills in return, bolstering your professional profile.

Stay Consistent:

Update Your Status: Regularly update your LinkedIn status with professional achievements, industry news, or relevant content to stay top-of-mind with your network.

Job Hunting Mode: Consider enabling "Job Seeker Preferences" in your profile settings, which signals to recruiters that you're open to new job opportunities.

Research Companies:

Company Insights: Use LinkedIn's company pages to research potential employers. You can learn about company culture, recent news, and the types of employees they hire.

Follow-Up:

Follow Up on Applications: After applying for a job, follow up with the hiring manager or recruiter to express your continued interest in the position. This demonstrates your enthusiasm and professionalism.

Skills Development:

Continuous Learning: Consider taking advantage of LinkedIn Learning, which offers a wide range of courses and certifications to enhance your skills and make you more marketable.

Networking Events:

Attend LinkedIn Events: Participate in LinkedIn's virtual events, such as webinars and networking sessions, to connect with professionals and learn from industry experts.

LinkedIn is a dynamic platform that can significantly impact your job search and career advancement. By optimizing your profile, actively networking, and staying engaged with your network and industry, you can increase your chances of finding, applying for, and ultimately winning the job opportunities you seek.

Part 3: Leveraging industry-specific resources

Each industry has its own unique resources and opportunities. To effectively navigate the job market, leveraging industry-specific resources is critical.

Start by identifying professional associations relevant to your field. These organizations often provide job listings, networking events, and industry insights. Membership provides you with valuable connections and knowledge.

Additionally, consider joining online forums and discussion groups focused on your industry. These platforms are great for participating in discussions, seeking advice and understanding industry trends. They can also be a place to find job information and connect with potential employers.

Don't overlook the power of your company's career page. Many organizations prefer to advertise their job vacancies on their website. Check your target company's careers page regularly for updates on new opportunities.

You can gain a competitive advantage in the job market by leveraging industry-specific resources and connecting with professionals who share your interests and goals.

These resources not only help you discover job opportunities, but also provide valuable insights and support to help you in your career.

Chapter 4: Crafting a Great Resume and Cover Letter

Part 1: Crafting a Great and Compelling Resume

Your resume is your primary tool for making a strong first impression with potential employers. A well-crafted resume can open doors to exciting career opportunities, while a poorly constructed one can close them. In this guide, we will walk you through the essential elements and strategies for creating a great and attractive resume that showcases your qualifications, experience, and skills effectively.

1. Choose the Right Resume Format:

Select a resume format that best suits your background and career goals. Common formats include:

Reverse-Chronological: Ideal for those with a strong work history in a specific field. It lists work experience in reverse chronological order, starting with the most recent position.

Functional: Suitable for career changers, those with employment gaps, or recent graduates with limited work experience. This format emphasizes skills and qualifications over chronological work history.

Combination/Hybrid: Combines elements of both chronological and functional formats, allowing you to showcase your skills while still providing a work history section.

2. Begin with a Strong Summary or Objective:

Your resume should start with a powerful summary or objective statement that succinctly communicates your career goals and the value you bring to potential employers. Tailor this section to each job application.

3. Include Contact Information:

Provide your full name, phone number, email address, and location. It's also common to include a LinkedIn profile if you have one.

4. Highlight Your Key Skills:

Create a dedicated section to showcase your core skills and qualifications. Be specific and focus on skills that are relevant to the job you're applying for. Use bullet points for clarity.

5. Detail Your Work Experience:

In the work experience section, list your previous jobs, starting with the most recent. Include the following for each position:

Job title

Company name and location

Employment dates (month and year)

Responsibilities and achievements

Use the CAR (Challenge-Action-Result) method to describe accomplishments.

6. Emphasize Achievements:

Use quantifiable achievements and results to demonstrate the impact of your work. Numbers and metrics stand out and provide evidence of your contributions.

7. List Your Education:

Include your educational background, starting with the highest degree earned. Include the institution's name, location, degree obtained, and graduation date. Mention any relevant certifications or awards.

8. Add a Relevant Professional Summary:

Incorporate a summary section that highlights your career accomplishments, areas of expertise, and key strengths. Use this section to demonstrate how you align with the job's requirements.

9. Tailor Your Resume for Each Application:

Customize your resume for each job you apply for. Use keywords from the job description and align your qualifications with the specific requirements of the role.

10. Utilize Action Verbs:

Begin bullet points with strong action verbs to describe your responsibilities and achievements. Action verbs add impact to your resume and make it more engaging.

11. Show Career Progression:

Highlight your career progression and development over time. Emphasize how your skills and responsibilities have evolved from one position to the next.

12. Include Relevant Volunteer Work or Projects:

If you have volunteer experience or side projects that are relevant to the job, include them in a dedicated section. This can demonstrate your passion and initiative.

13. Avoid Irrelevant Information:

Omit any information that is not directly related to the job or industry you are targeting. Personal details, unrelated hobbies, and excessive personal information should be left out.

14. Use a Professional Font and Format:

Choose a clean, easy-to-read font (e.g., Arial, Calibri, or Times New Roman) and maintain consistent formatting throughout your resume. Use headings and subheadings to make your document easy to navigate.

15. Proofread Thoroughly:

Proofread your resume carefully for grammatical errors, typos, and formatting issues. Errors can create a negative impression. Consider asking someone else to review it as well.

16. Keep It Concise:

Your resume should ideally be one page for those with less experience (0-5 years) and up to two pages for those with more extensive experience. Be concise and prioritize the most relevant information.

17. Demonstrate Cultural Fit:

Research the company culture and values, and ensure that your resume reflects your alignment with the organization's mission and goals.

18. Keep a Master Resume:

Maintain a "master resume" that includes all your skills, qualifications, and experiences. Customize it for each application, selecting the most relevant information.

19. Save in a Common Format:

Save your resume as a PDF or Word document to ensure compatibility with most application systems.

Part 2: Writing a Great Cover Letter

A well-crafted cover letter can be your key to unlocking the doors to your dream job. It's your chance to introduce yourself to potential employers, showcase your qualifications, and convey your enthusiasm for the position. In this guide, we'll explore the essential elements of a compelling cover letter that sets you apart from the competition and increases your chances of securing the job you're applying for.

1. Personalize Your Cover Letter:

One size does not fit all when it comes to cover letters. Each cover letter should be tailored to the specific job you're applying for. Address it to the hiring manager or recruiter by name, if possible. Personalization demonstrates your genuine interest in the role.

2. Start with a Strong Opener:

The opening paragraph should grab the reader's attention. State the position you're applying for and where you found the job posting. If you were referred by someone, mention their name, as referrals can carry weight.

3. Showcase Your Enthusiasm:

Express your genuine enthusiasm for the role and the company. Explain why you're excited about the opportunity and how it aligns with your career goals. Be specific and avoid generic statements.

4. Highlight Your Qualifications:

The body of your cover letter should focus on your qualifications and achievements. Use examples from your work experience, education, and skills that directly relate to the job requirements. Your goal is to convince the employer that you're the right fit for the role.

5. Provide Specific Examples:

Back up your claims with concrete examples of your accomplishments. Use the CAR (Challenge-Action-Result) method to explain how you addressed challenges and achieved positive outcomes in your previous roles.

6. Address Potential Concerns:

If you have any potential concerns, such as employment gaps or a career change, address them in a positive and confident manner. Use these situations as opportunities to demonstrate your adaptability and commitment.

7. Tailor Your Skills:

Align your skills with the job description. If the job posting mentions specific skills or qualifications, ensure that you discuss how you possess those skills in your cover letter.

8. Convey Cultural Fit:

Show that you are a good fit for the company culture. Research the company's values, mission, and culture, and highlight how your values align with theirs.

9. Be Concise and Clear:

Keep your cover letter concise and to the point. Aim for a length of about 250-400 words. Use clear and straightforward language to communicate your qualifications and intentions.

10. Use Keywords:

Incorporate keywords from the job posting into your cover letter. Many companies use applicant tracking systems (ATS) to screen applications, and using relevant keywords can help your application get noticed.

11. Address What You Can Offer:

Explain not only what you can gain from the position but also what you can contribute to the company. Show that you're not just interested in the job but in being an asset to the organization.

12. End with a Strong Closing:

The closing paragraph should reiterate your enthusiasm for the role and your desire to discuss how you can contribute further. Request an interview or express your eagerness to speak with the employer.

13. Use Professional Formatting:

Format your cover letter professionally. Use a standard font and a clean layout. Address your letter appropriately, and include your contact information at the top. Sign off with a professional closing.

14. Proofread Carefully:

Review your cover letter for spelling, grammar, and formatting errors. Mistakes can leave a negative impression, so take the time to proofread thoroughly.

15. Keep a Positive Tone:

Maintain a positive and professional tone throughout your cover letter. Avoid negativity, criticism, or complaints about your current or past employers.

16. Follow Submission Guidelines:

Adhere to the submission guidelines provided in the job posting. If the employer requests specific documents or formats, ensure that you comply with their requirements.

17. Consider Including a Postscript:

A postscript (P.S.) at the end of your cover letter can be an effective way to reiterate your interest or add a final compelling point.

18. Send a Thank You:

After submitting your application, send a thank-you email to express your gratitude for considering your application. It's a small but courteous gesture that can leave a positive impression.

19. Keep a Copy:

Retain a copy of your cover letter for your records. It can be helpful for reference during an interview or when preparing for follow-up communication.

20. Seek Feedback:

If possible, ask a trusted friend or colleague to review your cover letter. External feedback can provide valuable insights and help you make improvements.

A compelling cover letter is your opportunity to make a strong first impression and stand out in a competitive job market. By personalizing your letter, showcasing your qualifications, and demonstrating your enthusiasm, you can significantly increase your chances of landing your dream job.

Basic Cover Letter Template

Remember to customize it for each job application by addressing the specific company and job details:

[Your Name]

[Your Address]

[City, State, ZIP Code]

[Your Email Address]

[Your Phone Number]

[Date]

[Employer's Name]

[Company Name]

[Company Address]

[City, State, ZIP Code]

Dear [Employer's Name],

[Opening Paragraph]

I am writing to express my strong interest in the [Job Title] position at [Company Name], as advertised on [Job Board/Company Website]. With a proven track record in [Relevant Skill/Experience], I am eager to contribute my expertise and passion for [Industry/Field] to your team.

[Second Paragraph]

Throughout my career, I have consistently demonstrated my ability to [Highlight Key Achievement or Skill] and [Another Key Achievement or Skill], resulting in

[Quantifiable Outcome/Result]. This experience, combined with my strong [Relevant Skill], uniquely positions me to excel in this role. I am particularly drawn to [Company Name]'s commitment to [Company's Unique Value or Mission], and I am excited about the opportunity to contribute to your continued success.

[Third Paragraph]

What sets me apart is my dedication to [Company's Unique Value or Mission] and my drive to [Specific Goal Related to the Role]. I am confident that my [Relevant Skill/Experience] and [Relevant Skill/Experience] make me a strong fit for your team. Additionally, my ability to [Additional Skill or Trait] ensures that I can quickly adapt to new challenges and contribute to [Company Name]'s growth.

[Fourth Paragraph]

I am excited about the opportunity to discuss how my skills and background align with [Company Name]'s needs. Please find my resume attached for your review. I would welcome the chance to further discuss how my experience and passion for [Industry/Field] can contribute to [Company Name]'s continued success.

[Closing Paragraph]

Thank you for considering my application. I look forward to the possibility of speaking with you in more detail about how I can bring value to your team. You can reach me at [Your Phone Number] or via email at [Your Email Address].

Sincerely,

[Your Name]

This template provides a solid structure for your cover letter, but remember to customize it for each application. Highlight specific skills and achievements that match the job requirements and research the company to demonstrate your genuine interest. A well-tailored cover letter can significantly enhance your job application.

Part 3: Making your application ATS-friendly

In the competitive world of job hunting, applicant tracking systems (ATS) have become a ubiquitous tool for employers to manage and filter job applications. To increase your chances of getting noticed by potential employers, it's crucial to understand how ATS works and optimize your job application accordingly. In this comprehensive guide, we'll explore strategies for making your job application ATS-friendly and increasing your chances of securing your dream job.

Understanding ATS

Applicant tracking systems are software applications that help employers manage the recruitment process. They collect, organize, and filter job applications, enabling recruiters and hiring managers to identify the most qualified candidates efficiently. ATS is designed to streamline the hiring process, but it can be a challenge for job seekers to navigate unless they understand how it works.

ATS scans resumes and job applications for specific keywords, skills, and qualifications that match the job description. It then ranks candidates based on the level of alignment with the job requirements. Only the top-ranked candidates typically move forward in the hiring process. To ensure your application passes through ATS screening, follow these steps:

1. Tailor Your Resume:

Customize your resume for each job application. Analyze the job description carefully and identify the keywords and phrases used to describe the role and qualifications. Ensure your resume includes these keywords, particularly in the skills and qualifications sections.

2. Use Standard Resume Formats:

ATS is most compatible with standard, straightforward resume formats. Avoid using elaborate designs, graphics, or non-standard fonts, as they may confuse the system. Stick to simple, clean, and professional formatting.

3. Include a Summary Section:

Incorporate a summary or professional profile at the beginning of your resume. This section should provide a concise overview of your skills and qualifications, making it easier for ATS to identify your key strengths.

4. List Relevant Keywords:

In addition to using keywords from the job description, include other relevant industry-specific terms and phrases. However, do this organically and avoid keyword stuffing, which can negatively impact your application.

5. Focus on Skills:

Create a dedicated section in your resume to showcase your skills. Be explicit about your capabilities, ensuring they align with the job requirements. Use bullet points for clarity.

6. Specify Your Experience:

Detail your work experience, highlighting accomplishments and responsibilities relevant to the position you're applying for. Quantify your achievements wherever possible, as numbers and metrics stand out to ATS.

7. Education and Certifications:

List your educational background, certifications, and qualifications. Include the name of the institution, degree, graduation date, and any relevant certifications.

8. Use Proper Job Titles:

Use standard job titles that accurately represent your roles. ATS may not recognize creative job titles or abbreviations.

9. File Format:

When submitting your application electronically, use common file formats such as PDF or Word (.doc or .docx). These formats are most compatible with ATS.

10. Proofread and Format Check:

Before submitting your application, carefully proofread and check for formatting issues. Spelling and grammatical errors can negatively impact your application.

11. Customized Cover Letter:

Tailor your cover letter for each job application, incorporating keywords and phrases from the job description. A well-matched cover letter can enhance your application's ATS compatibility.

12. Be Mindful of Symbols:

Avoid using special characters, symbols, or non-standard punctuation in your resume or cover letter, as these may not be recognized by ATS.

13. Submit as Requested:

Follow the application submission instructions provided in the job posting. If the employer requests a specific format or method, adhere to their guidelines.

14. Check for Compatibility:

Ensure your application materials are compatible with mobile devices and various operating systems, as employers may access them from different platforms.

15. Save a Master Resume:

Maintain a master resume that includes all your skills, qualifications, and experiences. When applying for a job, customize this master resume to create a tailored version for the specific position.

16. Regularly Update Your LinkedIn Profile:

Many employers use LinkedIn to find potential candidates. Keep your LinkedIn profile updated with the same keywords and information you use in your job applications.

By implementing these strategies, you can significantly improve the ATS-friendliness of your job applications. Remember that while optimizing for ATS is essential, your application should also be compelling and tailored to human recruiters. Balancing these considerations will help you stand out in the job market and increase your chances of landing your desired position.

Chapter 5: Preparing for the Interview

Part 1: Anatomy of a Job Interview

Understanding the structure and purpose of a job interview is crucial to effective preparation. Interviews usually follow a general structure and can be broken down into a few key parts:

1. Introduction: The interview begins with a warm welcome and self-introduction. This is the time to make a positive first impression, which often involves a firm handshake and a friendly greeting.

2. Icebreaker questions: To build rapport, the interviewer can ask informal, non-job-related questions at the beginning of the interview.

3. Behavioral Questions: These questions are designed to assess your past behavior and how you handled specific situations. They often begin with phrases like "Tell me once..."

4. Technical Questions: For technical positions, you can expect questions that assess your knowledge and problem-solving abilities related to your field.

5. Case questions: These questions are common in consulting and analytical positions and require you to solve a hypothetical problem or case.

6. Ask the Interviewer Questions: Toward the end of the interview, you will have an opportunity to ask questions about the company, the position, and the team.

7. Closing: The interview usually ends with closing remarks from the interviewer, an invitation to ask any final questions, and acknowledgments.

Understanding this anatomy can prepare you to answer, ask questions, and make a strong overall impression.

Part 2: Type of interview: face-to-face, phone and video

Job interviews come in many forms, each with its own nuances and considerations:

Face to face interview:

• These traditional interviews require you to meet face-to-face with the interviewer at the company location.

• Dress professionally and be on time.

• Pay attention to body language, maintain eye contact, and shake hands confidently.

Telephone:

• Telephone interviews are often used for initial screening or when distance is a factor.

• Find a quiet, private place and use an open phone line.

• Use notes or resumes to quote key points from the conversation.

Video interview:

• Video interviews are increasingly common, especially for remote positions.

• Test your equipment (camera, microphone, and Internet connection) ahead of time.

• Wear professional attire and choose a well-lit, uncluttered interview location.

• Keep eye contact with the camera, not the screen.

Part 3: Research the company and role

One of the most critical aspects of interview preparation is to thoroughly research the company and the position you are interviewing for. Here are things to pay attention to:

Company research:

• Company History: Understand the background of the company, including its founding, growth and major milestones.

• Company Culture: Explore your company's values, culture and mission statement. Research its reputation as an employer.

• Recent News and Updates: Be familiar with the latest news, mergers, acquisitions or major achievements.

• Leadership Team: Get to know key executives and their backgrounds.

• Product or Service: Understand the company's products and how they fit into the market.

Interviews can be nerve-wracking, but with the right techniques and strategies, you can put your best self forward and leave a lasting impression.

1. Preparation is key:

• Thoroughly review the job description and company.

• Practice answering common interview questions.

• Prepare questions to ask the interviewer.

2. Use the STAR method:

• Situation: Describe the situation you were in.

• Task: Explain the task or challenge you face.

• Action: Detail the actions you took to resolve the situation.

• Results: Share a positive result or something you learned.

3. Be concise and clear:

• Keep your answers clear and concise and avoid overly long explanations.

• Use examples from your experience to illustrate your points.

4. Establish a connection:

• Build rapport by being friendly and approachable.

• Use positive body language, maintain eye contact, and give a firm handshake.

5. Showcase your soft skills:

• Emphasis on soft skills such as communication, problem solving and teamwork.

• Use real-world examples to demonstrate your proficiency.

6. Demonstrate cultural fit:

• Show that you identify with the company's values and culture.

• Discuss your experiences that reflect these values.

Part 4: Answer common interview questions

During the interview process, you may encounter a series of common questions. Here are ways to effectively solve some of these problems:

1. Tell us about yourself:

• Stay professional and focus on your career, skills and achievements.

• Tailor your answers to the specific job you are applying for.

2. What are your strengths and weaknesses?

• Highlight job-related strengths.

- When discussing weaknesses, explain how you are working to improve them.

3. Why do you want to work here?

- Express your enthusiasm for the company and the position.

- Mention specific reasons, such as the company's mission or industry reputation.

4. Describe a challenge you face at work

- Use the STAR method to build your answer.

- Focus on how you solved the problem and what you learned from it.

5. Where do you think you will be in five years?

- Describe how this position aligns with your long-term career goals.

- Emphasize your commitment to career development and contribution to the company.

6. Why should we hire you?

- Summarize the skills and experiences that make you an ideal candidate.

- Mention what makes you different from other applicants.

Part 5: Demonstrate your skills and experience

To really stand out in an interview, you must effectively demonstrate your skills and experience that make you an ideal candidate for the position:

1. Be consistent with the job description:

• Clearly link your qualifications to job requirements.

• Use specific examples to demonstrate your suitability for the position.

2. Quantify achievements:

• Use numbers and metrics to highlight your achievements.

• For example, "My sales revenue increased by 20% in the first quarter."

3. Emphasize relevant experience:

• Prioritize discussions of experience directly related to the job.

• Explain how your past roles prepared you for this position.

4. Become a problem solver:

• Demonstrate your problem-solving skills by discussing challenges you have overcome.

• Explain how you deal with complex problems and make decisions.

5. Highlight adaptability:

• Emphasize your ability to adapt to new situations or industries.

• Mention instances where you successfully induced change.

6. Show enthusiasm and commitment:

• Express your enthusiasm for the position and the company.

• Discuss your long-term commitment to contributing to the organization.

By using effective interviewing techniques, answering questions with confidence, and demonstrating your skills and experience, you can increase your chances of acing your interview and making a memorable impression on your recruiting team.

Chapter 7:
Assessing Company fit

Part 1: Determining Company Culture and Values
Assessing company fit is crucial to ensuring you not only get a job but that the job is right for you. Company culture and values play an important role in this assessment.

Determine company culture and values:

1. Research: Conduct in-depth research on the company. Explore their website, social media presence, and employee reviews on sites like Glassdoor. Pay attention to the language and tone used in their materials, as this can provide insight into their values.

2. Talk to current employees: If possible, reach out to current or former employees to get an insider's view of the company culture. You can learn a lot from their experience and insights.

3. Ask during the interview: During the interview, ask about the company's values and culture. This shows that you are genuinely interested in aligning with their ethos.

4. Trust your gut: Pay attention to how you feel during interviews and interactions with company representatives. Your intuition can often guide you in assessing whether the company culture resonates with you.

Asking the right questions during the interview is key to determining whether you are a good fit for the company. Here are some questions to consider:

1. What are the company's mission and core values?

• This question can help you understand the company's overall goals and the principles that guide its decisions.

2. Can you describe the day-to-day responsibilities of this role?

• This question gives you insight into your future job and whether it will meet your expectations.

3. What is the typical career progression for someone in this position?

• Understanding your potential career path within the company can help you gauge long-term suitability.

4. How does the company support professional development and growth?

• Understanding opportunities for advancement and skill development is critical to long-term satisfaction.

5. What is the company's approach to work-life balance?

• Evaluating the company's stance on work-life balance is critical to your well-being and long-term commitment.

6. How does the company promote diversity and inclusion?

• Asking about diversity and inclusion efforts can reveal a company's commitment to creating a welcoming and equitable workplace.

Part 3: Assessing long-term compatibility

Assessing long-term compatibility with a company requires a deep understanding of how your values, goals, and expectations align with the organization. Here's how to evaluate this:

1. Reflect on your values: Consider your own values, work style and priorities. Does the company culture support these elements or conflict with them?

2. Evaluate your goals: Examine your long-term career goals and determine whether the company offers opportunities for growth and advancement that match your ambitions.

3. Evaluate work-life balance: Evaluate the company's stance on work-life balance and whether it meets your personal needs and expectations.

4. Consider culture fit: Think about how well you would fit into the company culture. Are you satisfied with the way your organization works?

5. Analyze your happiness: Reflect on whether you can see yourself being truly happy and fulfilled in this role over a long period of time. Job satisfaction is crucial to long-term compatibility.

6. Trust your intuition: Sometimes, intuition can be a valuable guide. If something doesn't feel right, or you feel like you have a direct connection to the company, consider these gut feelings.

Assessing company fit is a two-way street. Just as the company evaluates your suitability for the position, you should also evaluate the company's alignment with your values and career aspirations. By asking the right questions and reflecting on your compatibility, you can make a more informed decision about your long-term commitment to the organization.

Chapter 8: Negotiating a Job Offer

Part 1: Understanding Compensation Packages

Before diving into the negotiation process, it's crucial to understand the components of your compensation package. Typical packages include:

1. Base Salary: This is your fixed, regular salary and usually makes up the majority of your income.

2. Bonuses and Incentives: Some positions offer performance-based bonuses or incentives that can significantly increase your earnings.

3. Benefits: Includes health insurance, retirement plans, paid time off and other benefits.

4. Stock options or equity: At some companies, you may receive stock options or equity as part of your compensation.

5. Additional benefits: These include flexible work arrangements, tuition assistance, or company discounts.

Part 2: Salary and Benefits Negotiation

Negotiating a job offer, including salary and benefits, is a delicate process. Here is a strategic approach:

1. Research market salaries: Research typical salary ranges for your position and industry. Sites like Glassdoor, PayScale, and industry-specific surveys can provide valuable data.

2. Know your value: Assess your skills, experience and unique qualifications. Be prepared to justify your request with specific examples.

3. Prioritize your needs: Determine which aspects of your compensation package are most important to you. This can help you focus on the negotiation.

4. Start with enthusiasm: Express your excitement for the job and interest in joining the company.

5. Wait for an offer: Don't raise salary issues until the employer has made an offer. Let them start negotiating.

6. Counteroffer gracefully: If the initial offer is lower than you expected, counteroffer professionally. Explain your reasons and express your willingness to be flexible.

7. Be willing to compromise: Understand that negotiation is a two-way street. Be prepared to make concessions to reach an agreement that benefits both parties.

Part 3: Legal considerations in job offers

Understanding the legal aspects of a job offer is critical to protecting your rights. Here are some key considerations:

1. Employment Contracts: Carefully review all employment contracts. Pay attention to clauses related to job responsibilities, non-compete clauses and intellectual property rights.

2. At-will employment: Understand the employment status because some jobs are "at-will," meaning either party can end the relationship at any time, with or without cause.

3. Nondiscrimination: Ensure job opportunities comply with nondiscrimination laws. Employers shall not discriminate on the basis of age, race, sex, religion, disability or other protected characteristics.

4. Benefits and policies: Be familiar with the company's benefits, policies, and employee handbook. This is crucial to understanding what the company offers and what to expect.

5. Salary transparency: Laws in some jurisdictions require employers to be transparent about salary ranges for specific positions. This is useful during negotiations.

6. Consider legal counsel: If you have complex or high-stakes negotiations, you may want to consult with an attorney who specializes in employment law for advice and review of the contract.

It is crucial to approach job offer negotiations with professionalism and a clear understanding of your values and needs. By knowing what to expect and understanding the legal aspects, you can obtain a compensation package that meets your expectations and legal rights.

Chapter 9: Using technology in your job search

Part 1: Online job boards and professional networks

In today's digital age, technology plays a vital role in job search. Online job boards and professional networks offer a wealth of opportunities and resources.

1. Online Job Board:

Online job sites like Indeed, Glassdoor, and LinkedIn Jobs are a treasure trove of job opportunities. Here's how to get the most out of them:

• Customized Search: Use advanced search filters to narrow your job search based on location, industry, job type and other relevant criteria.

• Job Alerts: Set up job alerts to be notified when new jobs that match your qualifications become available.

• Upload your resume: Many recruiting websites let you upload your resume, making it easier for employers to find you.

• Research Employers: Job boards often include company profiles, which can help you learn more about potential employers.

2. Professional network:

Professional networks, especially LinkedIn, provide a platform to connect with industry peers, showcase your skills and discover job opportunities:

• Build your network: Connect with professionals in your field, including colleagues, supervisors, and industry leaders.

• LinkedIn Profile: Build a compelling LinkedIn profile that highlights your skills, experience, and achievements. Added professional photos and detailed summary.

• Get active: Participate in LinkedIn groups and discussions to stay up to date on industry trends and network with potential employers.

Part 2: Build an Impressive LinkedIn Profile

LinkedIn is a powerful tool for job seekers, and an impressive profile is crucial. The establishment method is as follows:

1. Professional Photos: Use high-quality professional photos. A good headshot can make a positive first impression.

2. Compelling Title: Craft a title that succinctly describes your expertise and professional focus.

3. Detailed Summary: Write a well-structured summary that highlights your skills, achievements, and career goals. It should be engaging and informative.

4. Work Experience: List your relevant work experience, including job title, company, dates, and key responsibilities and accomplishments for each role.

5. Skills and recognition: Include relevant skills and seek recognition from those you relate to.

6. Recommendations: Ask for recommendations from colleagues, supervisors, and mentors to enhance the credibility of your profile.

7. Engage: Engage with your connections by sharing relevant articles, commenting on posts, and participating in discussions.

8. Portfolio and Projects: If applicable, showcase your work, projects, or publications to demonstrate your expertise.

9. Custom URL: Customize your LinkedIn profile URL to make it more user-friendly and professional.

Part 3: Using technology to understand situations

Technology can help you stay informed about job market trends, industry developments and potential opportunities:

1. Industry news websites: Subscribe to industry-specific news websites, blogs, and newsletters to stay informed about the latest trends and developments.

2. Google Alerts: Set up Google Alerts for keywords related to your industry or job search. You will receive email notifications when relevant news is released.

3. Social media: Follow industry-related accounts and hashtags on platforms such as Twitter and LinkedIn to obtain real-time information.

4. Professional forums and groups: Join online forums and groups related to your field. Sites like Reddit, Quora, and niche forums can be valuable sources of information.

5. Job Alert Service: Explore the Job Alert Service to get job listings based on your criteria delivered directly to your inbox.

6. Web Apps: Use web apps to connect with professionals in your industry. Platforms like Meetup and Eventbrite can help you discover relevant events and webinars.

7. Online Learning Platforms: Leverage online learning platforms like Coursera and LinkedIn Learning to acquire new skills and certifications.

8. Podcasts: Listen to industry-related podcasts to gain insights and knowledge from experts in your field.

By embracing technology, you can proactively stay informed, expand your network, and take advantage of the digital tools available to make your job search more efficient and effective.

Chapter 10: Resilience and Persistence

Part 1: Managing job search stress

Job hunting can be a stressful and challenging process. To effectively manage this stress:

1. Set realistic goals: Set achievable goals for your job search. This helps prevent feelings of being overwhelmed.

2. Time Management: Establish a structured schedule for your job search activities. This ensures you're making continuous progress while avoiding burnout.

3. Self-care: Prioritize self-care. Maintain physical and mental health by exercising regularly, maintaining a balanced diet and getting enough sleep.

4. Seek support: Rely on your support network, whether it's friends, family or a career counselor. Discussing your job search challenges can be cathartic.

5. Mindfulness and Relaxation Techniques: Practice mindfulness, meditation, or relaxation exercises to reduce stress and anxiety.

Part 2: Dealing with Rejection and Frustration

Job rejection can be a disheartening experience, and it's something that nearly everyone faces at some point in their career. Whether you're a recent graduate, changing careers, or simply seeking new opportunities, rejection is a normal part of the job search process. While it can be frustrating, it's essential to handle rejection in a way that preserves your confidence and resilience. In this guide, we'll explore strategies for dealing with job rejection and frustration.

1. Embrace Resilience

Rejection is part of the journey to success. It's essential to develop a resilient mindset. Instead of seeing rejection as a failure, view it as an opportunity for growth. Use it as a chance to learn and improve for future applications. Remember that many successful individuals faced numerous rejections before achieving their goals.

2. Self-Reflection

After receiving a rejection, take some time to reflect on the experience. Consider why you applied for that specific job and what you can learn from the rejection. Did you have the necessary qualifications? Did you effectively communicate your skills and experience in your application and interview? Self-reflection can help you identify areas for improvement.

3. Seek Feedback

Don't hesitate to reach out to the employer for feedback, especially if you've made it to the interview stage. Constructive feedback can provide valuable insights into what went wrong and how you can enhance your chances in the future. However, be prepared for the possibility that not all employers will provide detailed feedback.

4. Stay Positive

Maintaining a positive attitude is crucial. Remember that job rejection is not a reflection of your worth as a person. Avoid self-criticism and negative self-talk. Instead, focus on your strengths, achievements, and the qualities that make you a valuable candidate.

5. Stay Organized

Keep track of your job applications, interview details, and outcomes. This organization can help you identify patterns or areas where you might need improvement. It also ensures you don't miss follow-up opportunities with potential employers.

6. Keep Networking

Stay connected with your professional network. Informing your connections about your job search can lead to referrals and recommendations. Attend industry events, online webinars, and seminars to expand your network and learn about job openings.

7. Diversify Your Search

Explore different avenues for job searching. Look beyond job boards and consider reaching out to companies directly or working with recruitment agencies. Diversifying your approach can increase your chances of finding the right opportunity.

8. Skills Enhancement

Use the time between applications to enhance your skills. Consider taking courses, certifications, or workshops to make yourself a more attractive candidate. Continuous learning is a powerful tool for self-improvement.

9. Stay Active

Maintain a routine that includes physical activity and healthy habits. Exercise and a balanced diet can help manage stress and frustration. Staying active also boosts your energy levels, which is essential for a proactive job search.

10. Seek Support

Don't hesitate to lean on your support system. Share your frustrations and concerns with friends and family who can provide emotional support and encouragement. Sometimes, just talking about your experiences can be therapeutic.

11. Time Management

Structure your job search to be efficient and productive. Allocate time for research, applications, networking, and follow-ups. Staying organized and managing your time effectively can lead to better results and less frustration.

12. Set Realistic Expectations

Keep in mind that the job market can be competitive, and finding the right opportunity may take time. Adjust your expectations to ensure they are realistic and align with your skills and experience.

13. Focus on What You Can Control

Remember that some factors are beyond your control. Concentrate on aspects of your job search that you can influence, such as your application quality, interview preparation, and networking efforts.

14. Celebrate Small Wins

Acknowledge and celebrate small achievements along the way, such as receiving an interview invitation or making a valuable connection. Recognizing these milestones can boost your morale and keep you motivated.

In summary, dealing with job rejection and frustration is an essential part of the job search process. By developing resilience, learning from rejection, staying positive, and continually improving your skills and approach, you can navigate the challenges of job hunting and move closer to securing the right opportunity for your career. Remember, each rejection is a step toward finding the job that's the perfect fit for you.

Part 3: Staying motivated throughout the process

Job hunting can be a long process, and staying motivated is crucial to success:

1. Set clear goals: Define what you want to achieve during your job search. Having specific, achievable goals provides a sense of purpose.

2. Create a vision board: Visualize your desired results by creating a vision board containing images and goals related to your ideal job.

3. Break it down: Break your job search into smaller, manageable tasks. Every achievement can motivate you.

4. Stay organized: Maintain an organized job search system that records your applications, interviews, and follow-ups.

5. Stay informed: Keep up with industry trends and job market developments. This knowledge can inspire you to keep searching.

6. Actively build your network: Networking can be a motivating factor in your job search. Interact with professionals, attend events and make new connections.

7. Keep an open mind: Be open to unexpected opportunities and consider positions you may not have initially considered.

8. Reward yourself: Create a reward system for achieving milestones in your job search. Celebrate your achievements.

9. Seek guidance: If your motivation is waning, consider talking to a career coach or counselor who can provide guidance and motivation.

Remember, persistence and resilience are keys to a successful job search. Stay motivated, manage stress, learn from setbacks, and ultimately land a job that matches your career goals.

Chapter 11: Embracing Diversity and Inclusion

Part 1: The Benefits of a Diverse Workforce

Diversity in the workplace is more than just a buzzword; it's a valuable asset for both organizations and individuals:

1. Innovation and creativity: A diverse team brings different perspectives, resulting in more innovative problem solving and creative solutions.

2. Improved decision-making: When teams consider a wider range of factors and possibilities, diverse perspectives lead to better decisions.

3. Improved performance: Diverse teams tend to perform better than homogeneous teams, leading to higher productivity and better results.

4. Better attract and retain talent: An inclusive workplace attracts top talent, and employees are more likely to stay in an environment where they feel valued and included.

5. Reputation and Market Reach: Companies known for their diversity and inclusion practices generally have a better reputation and can reach a wider customer base.

6. Global Perspective: A diverse workforce can provide valuable insights into international markets and customer needs.

Part 2: Overcoming biases and overcoming challenges

When seeking a diverse and inclusive workplace, biases and challenges must be addressed:

1. Recognize Implicit Bias: Understand your own implicit biases and how they impact your decisions and interactions.

2. Education and training: Invest in diversity and inclusion training for employees at all levels to build awareness and understanding.

3. Inclusive Language: Promote the use of inclusive language in all communications and job descriptions to ensure everyone feels welcome.

4. Fair hiring practices: Implement standardized, fair hiring practices to minimize bias in the hiring process.

5. Diverse interview panels: Use diverse interview panels to evaluate candidates and reduce the risk of biased decisions.

6. Mentoring and sponsorship programs: Establish mentoring and sponsorship programs to support the career development of underrepresented employees.

7. Reporting mechanisms: Establish a clear and confidential reporting mechanism for employees to raise concerns about discrimination or bias.

Part 3: Looking for an inclusive employer

When searching for a job, it's important to identify employers who prioritize diversity and inclusion:

1. Research company practices: Investigate the company's policies and practices related to diversity and inclusion. Look for evidence of their commitment in their mission statements and annual reports.

2. Ask about employee resource groups: Ask if there are employee resource groups or affinity networks that support underrepresented communities.

3. Review inclusive benefits: Look for inclusive benefits such as family support programs, flexible work arrangements and gender-neutral facilities.

4. Company culture: Assess company culture through interviews or conversations with current or former

employees. Consider whether you feel a sense of belonging and inclusion.

5. Review diversity statistics: Companies committed to diversity often publish diversity statistics on their websites or in their annual reports.

6. Ask for feedback: Ask current or former employees about their experiences with diversity and inclusion within the company.

7. Review inclusion policies: Make sure the company has inclusion policies in place around recruiting, promoting and addressing discrimination.

When applying for a job, prioritize organizations that actively promote diversity and inclusion. Regardless of your background, these employers are more likely to provide you with an environment in which you can thrive.

Chapter 12: Preparing for the Future of Work

The world of work is evolving at an unprecedented pace, driven by technological advances, globalization and changing social expectations. In this chapter, we explore the changing nature of work, the skills and learning opportunities needed to thrive, and how individuals and organizations are adapting to remote and hybrid work environments.

Changes in the nature of work

The traditional 9-to-5 job in a brick-and-mortar office is no longer the norm. The nature of work has changed due to several key factors:

1. Technology: Automation and artificial intelligence are changing the work landscape. Routine tasks are increasingly automated, allowing employees to focus on more creative and strategic tasks. Work is becoming increasingly data-driven, requiring digital literacy and the ability to use emerging technologies.

2. Globalization: The rise of remote working and the ability to collaborate across borders means employees and organizations are no longer limited by geographic boundaries. Businesses can tap into a global talent pool and employees can explore new opportunities around the world.

3. The gig economy: The gig economy has grown significantly, providing workers with flexibility but also raising questions about job security and benefits. Freelance workers, independent contractors, and on-demand workers are reshaping the employment landscape.

4. Diversity and inclusion: Workplaces are becoming more diverse in terms of both gender and race. This shift is not just about meeting quotas, but about recognizing the value of diverse perspectives and experiences in driving innovation and solving problems.

5. Work-life balance: Employees are paying more and more attention to work-life balance. Remote work, flexible

schedules, and the ability to manage time are becoming fundamental considerations for many job seekers.

Skills and learning opportunities

As the nature of work changes, so do the skills needed to thrive in the modern workforce. Continuous learning is key and educational institutions, employers and individuals themselves must adapt to this new reality.

1. Digital literacy: Proficiency in digital tools and technologies is now an essential skill. This includes not only using software, but also understanding data analysis, cybersecurity and programming. Lifelong learning in this field is crucial.

2. Soft skills: While technology is critical, soft skills such as communication, emotional intelligence, adaptability, and problem-solving remain extremely valuable. They are essential for collaboration, leadership, and effectively navigating the changing workplace.

3. Critical thinking and creativity: Automation can handle everyday tasks, but humans are particularly suited to critical thinking and creativity. Encouraging these skills is critical to staying relevant and innovative.

4. Adaptability: The ability to quickly learn and adapt to new technologies and processes is a skill in itself. In the fast-paced world of work, it's crucial to be open to change and take on new challenges.

5. Lifelong Learning: Formal education is no longer a one-time event; it is a lifelong journey. Online courses, workshops and on-the-job training opportunities abound,

making it easier for individuals to upskill and reskill as needed.

Adapting to remote and hybrid work environments

The COVID-19 pandemic has accelerated the shift to remote work, with many organizations now adopting hybrid models that combine in-person and remote work. Adapting to these new work environments is critical for both employers and employees.

1. Technology and infrastructure: Remote work relies on stable network connections, secure communication tools, and remote access to company systems. Organizations need to invest in these technologies to effectively support their remote workforce.

2. Flexible work policies: Employers should have clear policies regarding remote and hybrid work, including expectations, communication guidelines and performance metrics. Flexibility is a two-way street, and trust is a key factor in making it work.

3. Mental health and well-being: Remote working can blur the lines between personal and professional life, potentially leading to burnout. Employers should prioritize mental health support, encourage breaks and promote work-life balance.

4. Team Building: Maintaining team cohesion in a remote or hybrid environment can be challenging. Organizations should invest in team-building activities, regular video meetings and other methods to foster a sense of belonging and collaboration.

5. Performance management: Remote and hybrid working require different approaches to performance management. Focus on results rather than micromanaging, and set clear expectations to ensure employees are productive and engaged.

6. Training and development: Ensure employees have access to training and development opportunities even in remote environments. Virtual seminars, webinars, and online courses can help employees gain new skills and stay up-to-date.

In summary, the future of work will be characterized by rapid change, driven by technology, globalization and changing social needs. To thrive in this dynamic environment, individuals must continually develop their skills and embrace digital literacy and soft skills. Organizations need to adapt to remote and hybrid work environments and foster a culture of flexibility, trust and well-being.

Chapter 13: Legal and Ethical Considerations for Job Applicants

As a job seeker, it is important to fully understand your rights, protect your personal information, and be aware of discrimination and unfair practices during the job search process. This chapter delves into these important legal and ethical considerations for individuals seeking employment.

Know your rights

Job seekers, like employees, have rights protected by various laws and regulations. Understanding these rights is critical to ensuring a fair and respectful job search experience.

1. Equal Employment Opportunity: Federal laws such as Title VII of the Civil Rights Act and the Age Discrimination Act protect job applicants from discrimination based on race, color, religion, sex, national origin, age, disability, or genetic information. Employment Act (ADEA) and Americans with Disabilities Act (ADA).

2. Right to privacy: Job seekers have the right to privacy, especially the right to privacy regarding their personal information. Employers must respect these rights and only request relevant information during the application process.

3. The right to a safe workplace: As a job applicant, you have the right to be free from violence, harassment, and unsafe working conditions. Employers must maintain a safe environment and job applicants should not tolerate any form of harassment during the application process.

4. Fair recruitment practices: Employers should follow fair and consistent recruitment practices. This includes using objective criteria to evaluate candidates, conducting thorough interviews, and providing equal opportunities to all applicants.

5. Reasonable Accommodations: If you have a disability, you have the right to request reasonable accommodations during the application process, such as modified interview formats or accessible application materials. The law requires employers to provide these accommodations unless it creates an undue hardship.

Protect your personal information

In today's digital age, job seekers must be vigilant in protecting their personal information during the job search process.

1. Resume and application information: Only information directly related to job application will be provided. Avoid giving out personal details, such as your Social Security number, until you have received a bona fide offer from a legitimate employer.

2. Online profile: Please be cautious about the information you share on social media and professional websites. Employers often search for candidates online, and the content you post may affect your job prospects.

3. Scams and phishing: Be wary of potential scams and phishing attempts. Legitimate employers will not ask you to provide sensitive personal information through unsecured channels. Please verify the legitimacy of the job opening and employer before sharing your profile.

4. Data Privacy Laws: Become familiar with the data privacy laws that protect your personal information. In some regions, such as the European Union, there are strict regulations, such as the General Data Protection

Regulation (GDPR), that govern how data is collected and processed.

5. Identity theft protection: Consider using an identity theft protection service to monitor your personal information and credit. These services can help detect and prevent identity theft, a risk that can be exacerbated during the job search process.

Recognize discrimination and unfair practices

Job seekers should be aware of potential discrimination and unfair practices during the job search process and know how to respond.

1. Discrimination: Be alert for any signs of discrimination, whether based on race, gender, age, religion or other protected characteristics. If you believe you have been discriminated against, document the incidents and consult with an attorney or appropriate agency.

2. Unfair Interview Questions: Employers should not ask questions about your personal life, marital status, religion, or other protected attributes. If you encounter an inappropriate interview question, you can politely refuse to answer or express your concerns.

3. Bait and switch job offers: Be wary of employers who make promises during the interview process but then fail to deliver upon hiring. Make sure verbal agreements or commitments are put in writing to protect your interests.

4. Unpaid Internships: Unpaid internships must meet certain standards allowed by law. If an internship primarily

benefits the employer without providing educational value to the intern, it may violate labor laws.

5. Misclassification: Employers may misclassify employees as independent contractors to avoid providing benefits and protections. Understand the criteria that distinguish employees from contractors and make sure you are classified correctly.

In summary, job applicants must fully understand their rights, be vigilant in protecting personal information, and be acutely aware of discrimination and unfair practices. While the job search process can be competitive and challenging, knowing and standing up for your rights is critical to a fair and respectful experience. If you encounter a legal or ethical issue during your job search, please consider seeking legal counsel or reporting the matter to the appropriate authorities. Your rights and dignity as a job applicant should be upheld and protected throughout the process.

Chapter 14: Strategies for Success

In a competitive job search environment, developing an effective strategy can make the difference between landing your dream job and overcoming ongoing challenges. This chapter explores key strategies for success, including developing a personalized job search strategy, leveraging connections and mentors, and setting goals to track your progress.

Develop a personalized job search strategy

A personalized job search strategy is crucial to standing out and ensuring you're targeting the right opportunities. The construction method is as follows:

1. Self-Assessment: Start by assessing your skills, strengths, weaknesses, values, and interests. What kind of work do you like and what are your career goals? Knowing yourself is the basis for developing a strategy.

2. Targeted job search: Focus on industries, companies, and roles that match your skills and career aspirations. Customize your resume, cover letter, and online profile to highlight your relevance to these specific opportunities.

3. Network: Use your network to uncover hidden job opportunities. Attend industry events, join professional organizations, and use online platforms like LinkedIn to network with professionals in your field.

4. Online Job Boards: While they can be helpful, don't rely solely on job boards. Customize your search, set up job alerts, and consider niche job boards that fit your industry.

5. Company Research: Research the companies that interest you thoroughly. Learn about their culture, values and latest developments. This knowledge can help you customize your application and perform better in interviews.

6. Skill Development: Invest in improving or acquiring the skills needed in your field. This may involve taking courses, certification or gaining practical experience.

7. Cover Letter and Resume Optimization: Create a compelling resume and cover letter that highlights your accomplishments and demonstrates how you contributed to the employer's success. Use keywords from the job description to make your application stand out.

8. Interview Preparation: Prepare for your interview by practicing frequently asked questions, researching the company, and asking thoughtful questions of your interviewer. Consider conducting a mock interview with a mentor or career coach.

9. Follow up: After your interview and application, don't forget to send a thank you note or email to express your interest and appreciation.

10. Persistence and adaptability: Finding a job can be a long process. Be persistent, adjust your strategy as needed, and be open to feedback and improvements.

Leverage the Internet and Mentors

Your professional network can be a valuable resource during your job search. Here's how to get the most out of it:

1. Networking events: Attend industry-specific networking events, career fairs, and conferences. These events

provide opportunities to meet and network with potential employers.

2. Online: Use professional social media platforms such as LinkedIn. Connect with former colleagues, mentors, and professionals in your industry. Share relevant content and participate in discussions to increase your visibility.

3. Informational Interviews: Seek out informational interviews with professionals in your field. These meetings can provide insights, advice, and potentially lead to job recommendations.

4. Mentoring: Consider finding a mentor who can provide guidance and support during your job search. Mentors can provide valuable advice, share their experiences, and help you navigate your career path.

5. Professional organizations: Join relevant professional organizations. These groups often provide access to industry-specific resources, networking opportunities, and recruiting websites.

6. Recommendations: If you have connections within a company that interests you, don't hesitate to ask for referrals. Employee referrals can be an effective way for you to get started.

7. Reciprocity: The Internet is a two-way street. Be willing to help others whenever possible as this breeds goodwill and can provide you with support when you need it.

Set goals and track progress

To keep your job search on track and stay motivated, it's crucial to set goals and monitor your progress.

1. SMART Goals: Use the SMART (Specific, Measurable, Achievable, Relevant, Time-Bound) framework to define clear and achievable goals. For example, "I apply to five relevant job postings every week."

2. Daily or weekly routine: Create a routine for your job search. Allocate specific time each day or week for activities such as researching companies, sending applications, and making connections.

3. Progress Tracking: Keep track of your job applications, interviews, and social interactions. Create a spreadsheet or use a job search app to track your progress.

4. Feedback and Adaptation: Ask for feedback from a mentor, advisor, or trusted peer. Use their insights to adjust your approach and improve your job search strategy.

5. Celebrate achievements: Recognize and celebrate small wins and milestones. Getting an interview or attending an information session is a significant accomplishment in your job search journey.

6. Maintain a positive attitude: Looking for a job can be all-consuming, but it's crucial to maintain a positive attitude. Focus on your long-term goals and remember that rejection is part of the process.

7. Self-care: Don't forget to take care of your physical and mental health. A balanced and healthy lifestyle will help you stay active during your job search.

In summary, a successful job search requires a well-thought-out strategy based on your skills and goals. Developing a personalized job search strategy, leveraging your connections and mentors, and setting and tracking your goals are key components to a successful job search. By following these strategies, you'll be better able to navigate the competitive job market and land a job that matches your desires and ambitions.

Chapter 15: Conclusion

As we wrap up this journey of job search and career development, it's time to summarize key takeaways to provide encouragement for your job search and help you prepare for your next career move.

Summary points

In this guide, we explore a wide range of topics related to your job search, from crafting a winning resume to acing an interview to adapting to a changing work environment. Here is a review of the important points:

1. Self-discovery: Understand yourself, your strengths, and career goals. Self-awareness is the foundation of a successful job search.

2. Resume and Cover Letter: Craft a compelling, customized document that highlights your skills, achievements, and the value you bring to a potential employer.

3. Job Search Skills: Use a variety of job search skills, including job boards, connections, and industry-specific resources.

4. Interview Preparation: Practice and prepare for the interview to showcase your skills, experience, and enthusiasm for the position.

5. Network and mentor: Leverage your professional network and consider seeking mentorship for guidance and support.

6. Adaptability: Embrace change and adapt to the changing nature of work, including remote and hybrid work environments.

7. Legal and Ethical Considerations: Know your rights as a job applicant, protect your personal information, and be alert to discrimination and unfair practices.

8. Goal Setting: Set SMART goals, track your progress, and stay positive throughout your job search.

Encourage you to find a job

Searching for a job can be a challenging and sometimes frustrating process. Remember you are not alone in this journey and success comes to those who persevere. Here are some encouragements to keep you motivated:

1. Resilience: Rejection is part of the job search process. Don't let setbacks define you. Learn from them, adapt and keep moving forward.

2. Continuous learning: The job market is dynamic, so you must continue to learn and grow. New skills and knowledge can set you apart from other candidates.

3. Support System: Rely on your support system, whether it's family, friends, mentors, or professional organizations. They can provide guidance, encouragement, and valuable insights.

4. Positive mindset: Stay positive and focus on your long-term goals. Visualize your successes and use setbacks as stepping stones to your next opportunity.

5. Respect your health: Take care of your physical and mental health. A healthy lifestyle is critical to maintaining the energy and resilience needed for a successful job search.

Get ready for your next career move

As you conclude this guide, it's important to look ahead to your next career move:

1. Reflect on your journey: Take some time to reflect on what you've learned and accomplished during your job search. Consider how your experiences have shaped your career aspirations.

2. Set new goals: Define your next career goals and the steps needed to achieve them. Whether it's a new job, a promotion, or a career change, having clear goals is crucial.

3. Continue to network: Networking is a lifelong endeavor. Stay connected with your professional network, attend industry events, and seek mentoring opportunities.

4. Skill Development: Continue to develop your skills and stay current in your field. Consider advanced training, certification, or additional education when necessary.

5. Pay attention to industry trends: Keep abreast of industry trends and predict changes in the job market. Being proactive and adapting to new developments can give you a competitive advantage.

6. Work-life balance: Maintain a healthy work-life balance as your career progresses. Avoid burnout and prioritize your health.

7. Celebrate achievements: Acknowledge your successes, no matter how small. Celebrating your achievements will boost your confidence and motivation.

Your job search and career are dynamic and full of opportunities for growth and success. Remember, every experience, whether positive or challenging, helps you grow personally and professionally. As you move forward, stay focused on your goals, adapt to changes, and stay resilient and positive. With sheer determination and an ongoing commitment to self-improvement, you'll be well-prepared for your next career move and the exciting opportunities that lie ahead. Your career path is a journey and you are the author of your own success story. Wish you success in your future career!

About the Author

Talha Sharif, the author of "Career Triumph," is a seasoned professional with a wealth of experience in the realms of talent acquisition and career development. With a successful career spanning several years, Talha Sharif has made a significant impact in both hiring and assisting employers in refining and optimizing their recruitment processes. As a dynamic individual who has been a driving force in the world of human resources, Talha Sharif brings a unique blend of expertise, insight, and innovation to the art of hiring and job seeking. His remarkable journey through the hiring landscape has allowed Talha Sharif to understand the intricacies of both sides of the hiring process – from identifying exceptional talent to guiding job seekers towards their career goals. Talha Sharif has played a pivotal role in shaping recruitment strategies for numerous employers, helping them not only find the right candidates but also establish efficient and effective hiring procedures. His contributions have consistently led to improved outcomes, reducing time-to-hire and ensuring that the best-fit candidates are welcomed into the workforce. Beyond his corporate success, Talha Sharif is deeply passionate about sharing knowledge and expertise. This book, "Career Triumph," is a testament to his commitment to empowering job seekers and employers alike. Inside these pages, Talha Sharif distills his extensive experience, offering invaluable guidance and strategies to help individuals navigate the ever-evolving job market and achieve career success. With his extensive track record of transforming hiring processes and enriching the careers of countless individuals, Talha Sharif continues to be a source of inspiration and wisdom in the field of talent acquisition. "Career Triumph" is a testament to his dedication to facilitating career excellence, making it a must-read for anyone seeking to excel in the world of work. Talha Sharif welcomes the opportunity to connect with readers, share insights, and assist in their journey toward career triumph.

www.ingramcontent.com/pod-product-compliance
Lightning Source LLC
Chambersburg PA
CBHW062238290526
45794CB00006B/2335